AF270364

History Jokes

Joe King

Abdo Kids Junior
is an Imprint of Abdo Kids
abdobooks.com

abdobooks.com

Published by Abdo Kids, a division of ABDO, P.O. Box 398166, Minneapolis, Minnesota 55439.
Copyright © 2024 by Abdo Consulting Group, Inc. International copyrights reserved in all countries.
No part of this book may be reproduced in any form without written permission from the publisher.
Abdo Kids Junior™ is a trademark and logo of Abdo Kids.

Printed in the United States of America, North Mankato, Minnesota.

052023

092023

 THIS BOOK CONTAINS RECYCLED MATERIALS

Photo Credits: Alamy, Getty Images, Shutterstock

Production Contributors: Teddy Borth, Jennie Forsberg, Grace Hansen

Design Contributors: Candice Keimig, Pakou Moua

Library of Congress Control Number: 2022946711
Publisher's Cataloging-in-Publication Data

Names: King, Joe, author.

Title: History jokes / by Joe King

Description: Minneapolis, Minnesota : Abdo Kids, 2024 | Series: Abdo kids jokes | Includes online resources
and index.

Identifiers: ISBN 9781098266066 (lib. bdg.) | ISBN 9781098266769 (ebook) | ISBN 9781098267117
(Read-to-me ebook)

Subjects: LCSH: Jokes--Juvenile literature. | Wit and humor--Juvenile literature. | History--Juvenile
literature. | Humor--Juvenile literature.

Classification: DDC 818.6--dc23

Table of Contents

History Jokes

Why is history like a

fruit cake?

It's full of dates.

What do you call a musician

who just looked at Medusa?

A rockstar!

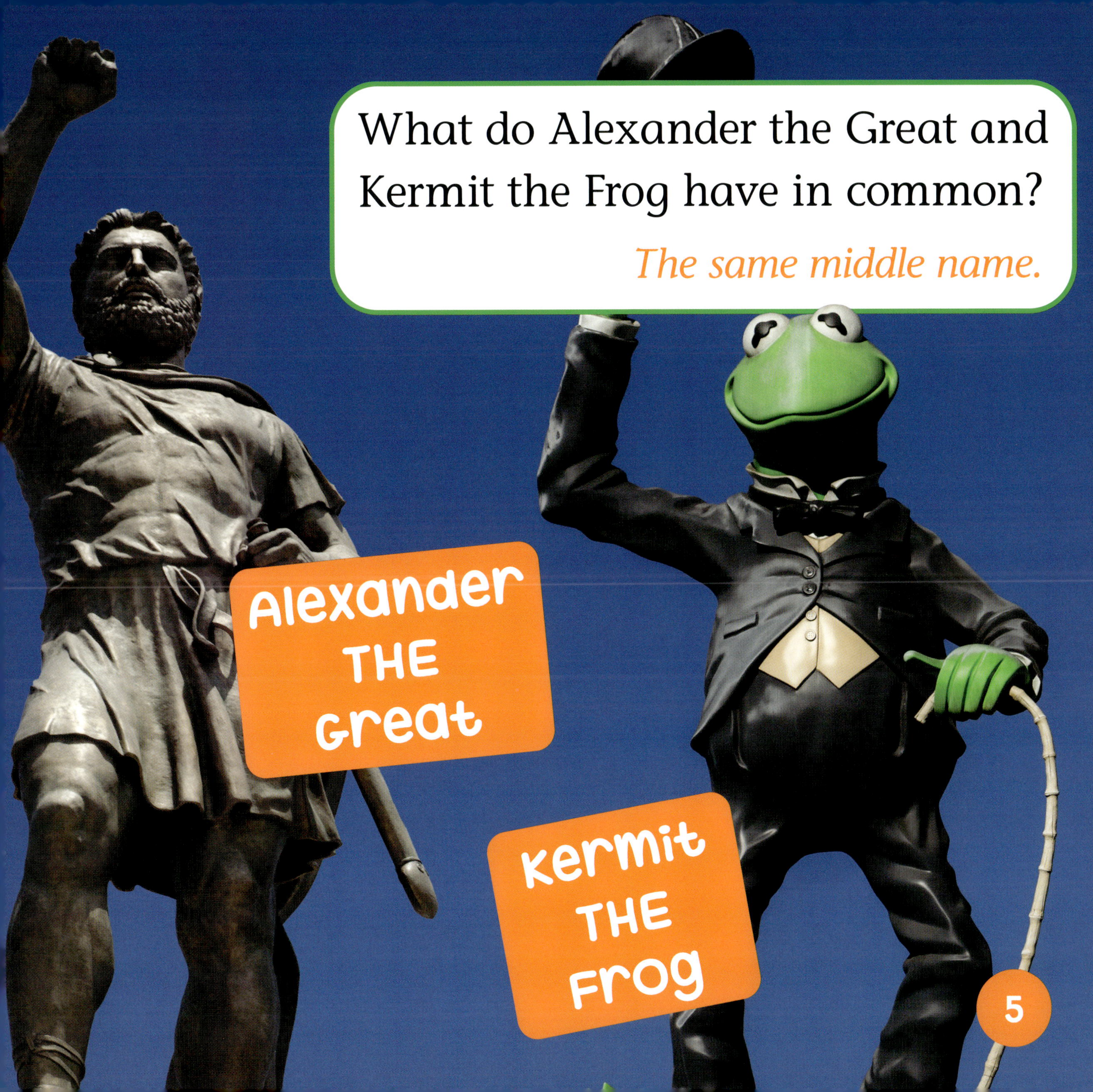

What do Alexander the Great and Kermit the Frog have in common?
The same middle name.
Alexander THE Great
Kermit THE Frog
5

Which famous Roman had bad allergies?

Julius Sneezer!

How did the Vikings send secret messages?

By Norse Code.

What's sweet, purple, and more than 5,000 miles long?
The Grape Wall of China!
What a grape joke!
7

What's an ancient Egyptian's favorite restaurant?

Pizza Tut!

What do you call a pharaoh that eats too many bean burritos?

King Toot.

When the Pharaoh asked his friend to join his business what did the friend say?

Let me sphinx about it. It could be a pyramid scheme!

What is a knight's

favorite fish?

Swordfish.

What do you call a

medieval knight who's

always sure of himself?

Sir Tainly!

Why is the Medieval Period often called the Dark Ages?
Because there were so many knights.
AHA!
HEH!
I've had JOUST about enough of this.
11

Why didn't the medieval

dragon like his birthday cake?

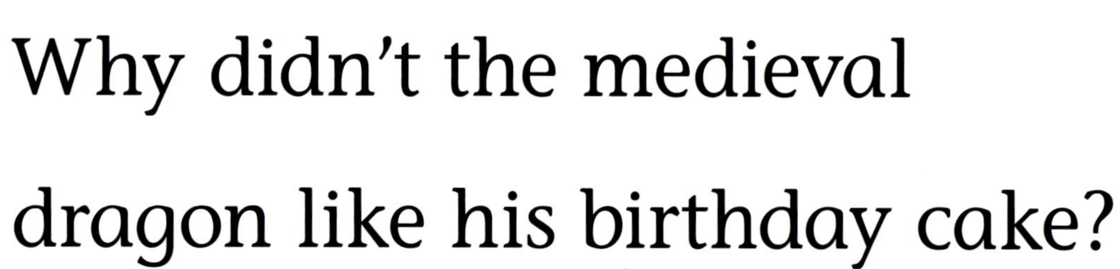

*It was too hard to blow out
the candles!*

Why was the king only 1 foot

tall?

He was a ruler!

Which one of King Arthur's knights built the round table?
Sir Cumference!
Get it??
circumference...
That joke was legendary.
13

Why did the British

cross the ocean?

To get to the other tide!

Why were the early

American settlers like ants?

They lived in colonies!

14

What did King George think of the American colonists?

He thought they were revolting!

Give me liberty or give me laughs!

15

Why did George Washington
have trouble sleeping?

Because he couldn't lie.

What did the Statue of Liberty
say as her visitors left?

Keep in torch!

16

What does the Statue of Liberty stand for?

Because she can't sit down!

Give me your riddles,
your puns,
your clever jokes...

17

Where was the Declaration
of Independence signed?

At the bottom!

What dance was very
popular in 1776?

The Indepen-dance!

18

Did you hear the joke
about the Liberty Bell?
It cracked me up!
Freedom rings!
PROCLAIM LIBERTY
HOUSE IN PHILADA BY ORDER OF THE A
PASS AND STOW
PHILADA
MDCCLIII
19

What did Benjamin Franklin
say when lightning hit his kite?

That was lit.

What did Shakespeare say
after completing his play
Romeo and Juliet?

Thine is lit.

20

Two wrongs don't make a right.
But two Wrights do make an airplane!
HOW DO I land this thing?!
JUST Wing it!
21

Joke-Telling Tips!

• Know your audience

• Timing is everything

• Confidence is key

• Go out on a high note!

22

Glossary

pun

a joke using a word that sounds like a different word or has another meaning. Examples from this book are "torch" (touch) and "Sir Tainly" (certainly).

thine

a very old word used in classic literature that means "that which belongs to thee" or "yours"

Index

Visit **abdokids.com** to access crafts, games, videos, and more!